C000299010

A BOOT UP

SHROPSHIRE HILLS

Bob Caddick & Bob Alton

First published in Great Britain in 2010

Front cover: *Willstone Hill*.

British Library Cataloguing-in-Publication Data
A CIP record for this title is available from the British Library

ISBN 978 1 906887 72 8

PiXZ Books
Halsgrove House, Ryelands Industrial Estate,
Bagley Road, Wellington, Somerset TA21 9PZ
Tel: 01823 653777
Fax: 01823 216796
email: sales@halsgrove.com

An imprint of Halstar Ltd, part of the Halsgrove group of companies
Information on all Halsgrove titles is available at: www.halsgrove.com

Printed and bound in China by Toppan Leefung Printing Ltd

Contents

How to use this book

Shropshire is England's largest land-locked county. It is also one of the nation's most rural and sparsely populated areas. To the west are the hilly borderlands with Wales, while to the north lie the richer agricultural acres of the Shropshire plain.

About a quarter of the county - mainly in the hill country to the south - was one of the first areas to be designated as an Area of Outstanding Natural Beauty in 1958. So it's not surprising that this often little-discovered and comparatively unheralded countryside is a real treasure for walkers.

The more obvious hill country does lie to the south and west of the county. But fascinating hill-tops also pop up further north and in the eastern parts of this varied district which offer the walker a very worthwhile outing. In fact Shropshire really does have hills to suit every rambler. From the highest summit of Brown Clee to the much more diminutive Lyth Hill and the gentle rolling countryside around Cleobury Mortimer, this is a landscape of ever-changing views, small character towns and villages which seem to have escaped ravages of time and have a heritage to engage even the most ardent fan of history and folklore.

Here you can walk all day and most times not meet another soul. Sit on a hill-top to savour not only your picnic but the view over a timeless landscape, thoughts interrupted only by the meowing cry of a high-circling buzzard or the bleat of a sheep. Stand on an airy summit which Bronze Age people chose as a place of burial and their Iron Age successors built a hill fort. Tread the footsteps of lead miners and quarrymen whose legacy has largely been reclaimed by nature - but look around and signs of industrial activity remain to add further interest to the walk.

The ten circular walks in this book have been chosen to give the walker a flavour of what lies in store for those who seek out the rural treasures of Shropshire. The walks vary from easy to the more challenging - but nothing too demanding. Most of the gradients are fairly easy on the knees and most paths are well walked. The price of solitude, however, is sometimes the fact that paths in more remote areas are not always well defined on the ground.

While the written descriptions for each walk should be sufficient to guide the walker round the route, the addition of the appropriate Ordnance Survey map is an essential part of any walker's kit. Recommended maps are given in the fact file for each walk.

These 10 walks are not set in particularly remote or wild countryside. Some, however, do pass through somewhat exposed parts - Brown Clee, Hope Bowdler Hill, Mucklewick and Flenny Bank in particular - so go prepared with a waterproof, hat and gloves (in winter) and always wear boots. A rucksack for a snack and drink is also a good idea.

Public transport

For public transport details contact the following: Traveline West Midlands 0871 200 22 33. Shropshire Council Customer Services 0345 678 9006. Some areas are served by a weekend shuttle bus: www.shropshirehillsshuttles.co.uk More information is available on council website: www.shropshire.gov.uk/traveltransport.nsf

Key to Symbols Used

Level of difficulty:
Easy

Fair

More challenging

Map symbols:

🚗   Park & start

────   Tarred Road

-----   Footpath

■   Building / Town

+   Church

🍺   Pub

🍽   Café

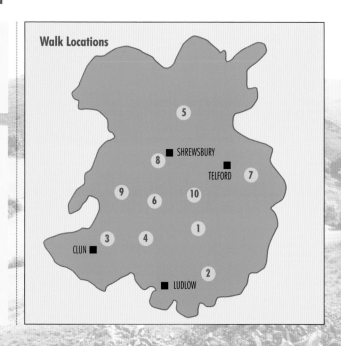

Walk Locations

5

8 ■ SHREWSBURY

■ TELFORD   7

9   6   10

1

3   4

CLUN ■

2

■ LUDLOW

1 Brown Clee and Burwarton

Climb the highest hill in Shropshire to savour panoramic views before descending through a country estate to the stone-built village of Burwarton with its Georgian pub.

Brown Clee has two summits - Abdon Burf the higher at 540 metres and its neighbour Clee Burf standing at 520 metres. (Burf is Saxon for fort.) The hill has been the scene of activity for 6,000 years. More recently - 3,000 years ago - Bronze age people decided that Abdon Burf would be an ideal spot for burials and in the Iron Age a hill fort was built. South from the summit can be seen another hill fort which has been well preserved on Nordy Bank. Fast-forward to the 1900s and the hill was the spot for the mining of coal and ironstone the remnants of which can be seen all around the summit. Today the hill plays a technical role with the latest communication equipment. The descent takes in part of the Burwarton estate of Lord Boyne.

Level: 🥾 🥾 🥾
Length: 6 miles
Start: Picnic site on minor road - signed Abdon and Tugford - on eastern flank of Brown Clee about a mile and quarter west of Cleobury North off B4364 Bridgnorth - Ludlow road. Grid ref SO608872.
Parking: Parking areas on eastern side of the lane.
Terrain: Walk sets out with one long sustained, but gradual, ascent. Eventual descent is also very gradual. Estate roads and roadside pavement.
Nearest refreshments: Boyne Arms at Burwarton 01746 797214. Howard Arms in nearby Ditton Priors 01746 712200.
Recommended map: OS Explorer 217.

Map labels:
- Abdon Burf
- Brown Clee Hill
- Boyne Arms
- Burwarton
- House
- Former Church
- Pool
- 1, 2, 3, 4, 5, 6, 7
- 00 m

1 From roadside parking go through the bridle gate on signed forest trail which bends right and heads uphill. The path enters woodland and meets a forest road. Go left for a short distance.

2 At marker post go right through pedestrian gate and ascend on well-defined path to pass through a gateway into open access land. Go forward, crossing a track, on a path making a gradual ascent. The final stretch involves a short steeper climb to join a service road. Go left to the summit.

3 At the toposcope, with masts right, go left down first set of steps then turn right to walk forward on gentle descent on Shropshire Way

Pine trees on Brown Clee

Brown Clee summit

towards facing fence-line. At the fence, at a marker post, turn left and ahead keeping fence right. When fence goes right continue forward on a wide grassy path heading towards a line of trees to arrive at a gate. (Short detour left just before the gate, arching back uphill, is a plaque in memory of 23 airmen killed in flying accidents.)

4 Pass through the gateway and go ahead bearing slightly left then forward on a gentle ascent to join left-hand boundary with trees left. At the wood corner go left over a fence-stile and walk forward. Pass through a gateway and go right on a track to Boyne Water. At the pool go left at a marker post and walk forward keeping water right. The path goes ahead between wire fencing.

Brown Clee has got itself into the pages of aviation history as it is thought there were more wartime air crashes here than on any other hill in Britain. A memorial now commemorates the 23 Allied and German airmen killed when their planes crashed into the hill in the Second World War.

Sheep on Brown Clee

Woolly fence near Burwarton

When this ends continue forward towards trees. The path eventually bears right touching the tree-line as it starts a descent.

(5) Pass through a gateway and go forward down a slope towards tree-line on the right. Continue downhill keeping fence right. When this fence slants right continue ahead with a small fenced fir coppice over to your left veering slightly right to meet an estate road opposite a stile and marker post at conifer enclosure. (The walk can be shortened by going left and keeping road back to start). Climb the stile and go forward through the coppice and down a field with Burwarton House left - gradually bearing left to join the fence walking to field bottom left-hand corner to road.

The original parish church of Burwarton lies in ruins and its replacement, also dedicated to St Lawrence built in 1877, was declared redundant in 1972 and is now a private house.

(6) Cross carefully and through gateway, immediately going left through another gateway. Go half right down the field aiming for right-hand corner of garden wall of the former Burwarton church - now a house. At the wall corner veer right and walk towards a gate at bottom

left-hand corner. Before reaching the gate seek out a stile on the left. Cross this and go half left up through graveyard. Pass through a gateway and go forward along the bottom of a lawn to the road.

(7) Cross and go right on the pavement to the Boyne Arms after which pass a road to Aston and Botterell and immediately before school sign go left through a pedestrian gateway. Head up field boundary. Continue forward on gradual ascent as the walk joins an estate road - ignoring all roads off left. At a road junction bear right and continue forward keeping to the road back to the start.

Service road on Brown Clee

The Boyne Arms

2 **Cleobury Mortimer and Mawley Hall**

From paths over rolling hills enjoy wonderful views of lush countryside, walk by a river which marks the boundary between two counties and tread estate tracks of 18th century Mawley Hall.

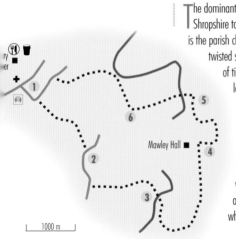

Mawley Hall ■

1000 m

Level: 🥾 🥾
Length: 4.5 miles
Start: The parish church at Cleobury Mortimer. Grid ref SO674758.
Parking: Car park on Childe Road signed off the main street. Grid ref SO673758.
Terrain: Undulating on field paths, tracks and a quiet lane.
Nearest refreshments: Pubs, café in Cleobury Mortimer.
Recommended map: OS Explorer 218.

The dominant feature of the little south Shropshire town of Cleobury Mortimer is the parish church of St Mary with its twisted spire - caused by warping of timbers. The walk quickly leaves the town to make the first gentle ascent with a backward look over the delightful jumble of architecture. It's then on to the site of what was once a forge at a weir on the River Rea which further downstream marks the boundary between Shropshire and Worcestershire. The walk now follows a clear track on a gradual ascent through the Mawley Hall estate with sightings of the house built in 1730.

1 With your back to the church walk down Lion Lane. When the lane bends sharp left, at Old Cider House, keep forward through a kissing gate. Veer half-left up the field to pass through gateway in top left-hand corner. Go ahead, keeping farm buildings left. Cross stile and go forward, ignoring footpath left, to follow the field left-hand boundary to a climb a stile in bottom corner. Go ahead down to cross a stream to exit on to a road.

The eighteenth century privately-owned Mawley Hall which looks out over the Rea valley, built for a Sir Edward Blount, is said to contain one of the finest Baroque interiors of any property in England.

Mawley Hall

4 Turn right on the driveway and at the first junction of tracks, go left on a footpath which runs downhill with walled garden, left. At the bottom of the garden keep the track as it follows the wall left. Within a short distance the track swings sharp right and the narrow bridleway (marker post) goes off right to descend through woodland.

2 Go right uphill keeping the lane for about a quarter of a mile, cresting the rise to go left on an unmade road. Go ahead to pass stables at Rookery Farm after which keep forward on a track and a view of Mawley Hall up to the left. The route leads down to a ford at the River Rea and site of a forge.

3 Turn right to cross footbridge and rejoin the estate track which, after a short distance, bends left. Ignore footbridge and then a track right and continue on the main track which makes a long steady ascent to Mawley Hall, to your left. Pass hay barn and continue forward - ignoring stile right - to the hall drive.

Today the Rea valley is a tranquil spot, but like many a river the Rea was a source of power and once the area resounded to the sound of forges and mills fed by the locally-mined iron ore and coal.

Cleobury meadow

(5) When the ground levels out, with the river on your left, ignore a path at sharp left turn and within a short distance go left to cross a footbridge. Go forward up the field left-hand boundary. Climb a stile and walk straight ahead, fence left. Keep forward over another stile

(6) At a metal gate, left, and waymarks, with chicken house beyond, veer half right down a path to climb stile at the river bank. Go ahead on riverside path to exit onto a lane at Cleobury Mill. Do not follow the road, but go left up a signed bridleway, through gateway to pass immediately left of the house to follow a sunken green lane to emerge onto an unmade road. Keep forward to exit onto a lane at Mortimer Hill.

Cleobury weir

Go right on the road. At a junction turn left downhill along Lion Lane to retrace steps.

*Cleobury Mortimer's
twisted spire*

3 **Clun and Bury Ditches**

Wonderful views of the Clun Valley, starting at Housman's poetic town.

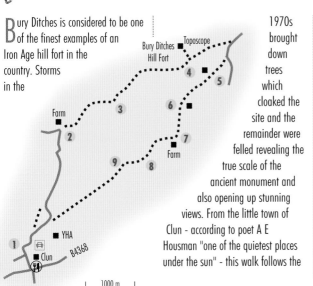

Level: 🥾 🥾 🥾
Length: 6.25 miles
Start/parking: Clun Memorial Hall car park signed from the main street. Grid ref SO302812.
Terrain: Field and woodland paths and tracks. One long but gradual ascent and steady descents. One short descent is on an awkward path. Quiet lanes. Two stream crossings which can be muddy after heavy rain.
Nearest refreshments: Choice in Clun.
Recommended map: OS Explorer 202 and 216.

Bury Ditches is considered to be one of the finest examples of an Iron Age hill fort in the country. Storms in the 1970s brought down trees which cloaked the site and the remainder were felled revealing the true scale of the ancient monument and also opening up stunning views. From the little town of Clun - according to poet A E Housman "one of the quietest places under the sun" - this walk follows the Shropshire Way on a steady ascent to Bury Ditches. The return has the added delight of wonderful views of the Clun valley.

19

Bury Ditches

From car park go left on the lane to pass the YHA. At Lake House continue forward on Shropshire Way up a track. At Mill Barn go right on enclosed path to cross a stile going half left over a field. Climb a stile and go ahead bearing slightly left to cross corner stile to rejoin the road and go left.

At a farm - Guilden Down - take the right-hand fork to go ahead between buildings and keep the road signed Bury Ditches - ignoring bridleway left. At a cottage bear left as the surfaced lane gives way to an unmade road and track. Pass through a barrier before embarking on the next climb as the route enters woodland. Ignore crossing path and when our path joins a surfaced forest road bear right to continue the ascent ignoring all initial roads and paths off.

As the ground levels out, at a fork in the forest road and waymark, veer left on a roadway - again ignoring paths off. At a major fork on crest of a rise go right - keeping Shropshire Way. Soon the contours spread out and on the left, through trees, can be seen the lip of Bury Ditches hill fort.

4 Pass through gateway and head up the grassy track which veers right to pass through the hill fort centre. As the path levels off, at a waymark post, go left to a topo-scope. Retrace steps to the main path and turn left to head downhill keeping to the main path to a picnic site and car park. Go out to the road and go right. Within a short distance part company with the Shropshire Way and go ahead on the lane. At a gentle left-hand curve, when woodland ends, go right through a gateway and ahead on a track with hedge and wood right.

5 On the approach to a cottage - Dawes Lines out of sight round bend to the right- go left through a pedestrian gateway.

Bury Ditches wood carving

Immediately turn right and ahead through a second gateway to go ahead along a shelf in the slope with the cottage up to your right. When this route bears right up towards a barn veer off left and ahead gradually slanting down the rather awkward steep slope to another pedestrian gate

Poet and English classical scholar Alfred Edward Housman, best known for his cycle of poems entitled A Shropshire Lad was, infact, not a Shropshire lad - but a lad from neighbouring Worcestershire.

with stream left. Go forward keeping to field bottom edge to eventually fol-low a fence forming boundary to house garden.

6 When this fence ends go left to cross a stream. Go ahead up the slope bearing right to continue the ascent on a farm road - woodland to the right. Now keep this road to Stepple Farm.

Clun

of the trees eventually going right to emerge into a field.

9 Go ahead on field right-hand boundary, hedge right. Keep forward keeping to a sunken path

7 At farm buildings veer right through the yard to pass in front of the house and ahead over a stile/gateway. Go forward on a track - ignoring a lower track. Pass through gateway and continue forward ignoring a grassy track slanting up to the right. Keep the lower route which descends through a gateway.

8 Go ahead to follow wheel tracks to ford a stream at a line of trees. Go ahead up the field towards Radnor Wood slanting slightly right to pass through corner gateway at woodland edge. Continue the ascent with wood immediately left. In top corner go left and then right up the bridleway on the inside edge

Clun

At least once a year Clun is most certainly not "one of the quietest places under the sun" when it stages the Green Man Festival. Based on a pagan festival the Green Man is said to be a "symbol of man's union with nature".

after which continue the descent on a field edge followed by a tree-lined sunken green lane. Cross footbridge and when the lane bends right go left over a stile to go half right and ahead over a field, cross plank footbridge and stile and ahead to exit on to a road. Go left back to start.

Clun doorway

Clun and Bury Ditches

Clun town hall

4 Craven Arms and Stokesay

Despite the relatively gentle nature of this walk there are some splendid views over the valley of the River Onny with an added bonus of seeing what is said to be the best preserved medieval fortified manor house in England.

Stokesay Castle is in reality a fortified manor house. Together with its timber-framed gatehouse and twelfth-century neighbouring church, it is truly an unforgettable sight. The house - now in care of English Heritage - has remained undamaged and largely unaltered since it was built in the thirteenth-century by a local wool merchant. From the Discovery Centre the walk ambles by the side of the River Onny before passing Stokesay to gently take to more elevated ground which provides splendid views of the castle and surrounding hills. A forest track gives a change of scene before returning to open country with views of the distant Titterstone and Brown Clee hills. On the facing horizon

Level: 🥾
Length: 3.25 miles
Start: Shropshire Hills Discovery Centre just off A49 on southern edge of Craven Arms. Grid ref SO434827. Additional parking on Corvedale Road.
Terrain: Gentle gradients on riverside path, field paths and forest track. Some paths may be over cultivated land. Busy road crossings and short stretch on pavement and quiet lane.
Nearest refreshments: Discovery Centre.
Recommended map: OS Explorer 217.

beyond Craven Arms can be spotted a stone tower sitting on top of Callow Hill. This is Flounders Folly built by local landowner Benjamin Flounders in 1838 and recently restored.

Craven Arms

Discovery Centre

① 🚗 🍴 ②

A49

Railway

⑥

River Onny

Stokesay Castle

⑤ ④ ③

ouse ◼

| 1000 m |

25

Riverside ramble

1 From the car park walk to the left of the Discovery Centre on path which is soon signed Onny Meadows and Riverside Ramble. At junction go left, keeping to the Riverside Ramble route, through a kissing gate and ahead on an unmade road, going right at a fork to cross the River Onny.

2 Go half right over the field, to fork right over a plank foot-bridge and up a slope to go ahead with fence on your right. Cross corner stile, go left and forward on a narrow path with fence left and the river down below. Cross fence-stile and go ahead on field boundary as the route joins the river. Climb a stile and go half left, cross stile, right, and up steps at top of which turn left on old road.

3 Carefully cross A49 to pavement and go right and turn left on lane to Stokesay. Pass church and castle ignoring first path right keeping to the road with a pond on your right at end of which turn right through double gates to go ahead on a farm track with barn left.

4 Cross railway line and go forward up a track and through a gateway. Go ahead through a field bearing slightly right to climb a facing stile. Continue forward to cross another stile and ahead continuing the gentle ascent to climb a stile at the boundary of Stoke Wood. Go ahead a short distance to go right to follow a forest road to a house - Clapping Wicket.

5 Pass through a kissing gate and turn right over a stile and within a few paces turn right, as indicated by a finger post (Three Woods Walk), to go half left crossing field diagonally to a stile. Continue on the same line to cross a stile. Go right on the field edge keeping fence on your right. Climb corner stile and continue ahead down field boundaries to pass

Secret Hills Centre

the road bends right go left on a surfaced footpath to cross A49 to Discovery Centre.

War Memorial at Stokesay

through corner gateway with clump of trees and ruined cottage left.

6 Go half left over field and at the edge (finger post) cross facing stile and go ahead down field boundary. At hedge corner go right to climb a stile and ahead down a sunken green lane to Craven Arms. Turn right on an estate road and when

Stokesay Castle

5 Grinshill and Corbet Wood

Walk through woodland on ancient sunken pathways and climb to the summit of the sandstone ridge of Grinshill Hill to enjoy a wonderful view.

Since the days of the Romans the hard sandstone from Grinshill Hill has been quarried and used in the construction of countless fine buildings throughout the land. This walk follows old pathways worn out of the stone and passes quarry faces which have long been recognised as being of geological importance. From the hill summit there are wonderful views south looking out over the county town and to the Wrekin, to Long

Level: 🥾🥾
Length: 3 miles
Start: Corbet Wood car park signed off A49 at Preston Brockhurst north of Shrewsbury. Grid ref SJ525238.
Terrain: Climb up Grinshill Hill is steep in places on uneven paths - but nothing too demanding. The descent is very gradual and easy. Remainder of the walk is on good bridleways and woodland paths.
Nearest refreshments: The Inn at Grinshill 01939 220410.
Recommended map: OS Explorer 241.

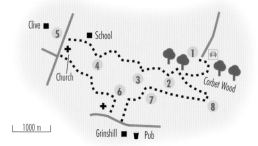

Mountain and the Breiddens. The descent to the village of Clive is via a delightful sunken stone-flagged path known as The Glat.

(1) In the car park walk back towards entrance and immediately before an old stone building go right on a footpath, going right at a fork, to go down a sunken path which curves right with the car park immediately up to your right. At a junction (the walk returns here) veer right and go ahead ignoring a path leading to rock face, right, and two paths off left.

(2) Within a short distance, at a marker post, bear right on a footpath which makes an ascent. Pass the end of a fence coming down the slope, right, and at a fork go left. Keep forward on a narrow and uneven path cut into the side of the slope. Ignore a path downhill and continue ahead as the ascent gets steeper to

Jubilee Oak

arrive at a break in the trees on the left and a viewpoint.

(3) With your back to the view walk forward to take the short right-hand path up the slope. At the top turn left and go ahead, keeping forward at a fork, as the climb gets

steeper. When the ground levels out - with a short section of wire fence right - follow the path as it curves left and ahead. At a fork veer right to meet a wider path. Turn left to the summit.

(4) With your back to the view go forward to pass immediately left of beacon to take the left-hand path. At a fork keep ahead on main path. When the path meets a track go left and ahead to pass a school to follow a sunken path to Clive church.

5 At the church go left on the road as far as the end of the churchyard wall to turn left on a track.

Jubilee Oak plaque

Clive church

Near Grinshill

The red illuminated beacon which sits on the summit of the hill is there as a warning to the helicopter pilots at nearby RAF Shawbury where trainees have included both Prince William and Prince Harry.

Go forward on the enclosed byway along the base of Grinshill Hill, passing an animal rescue centre.

6 At the village hall and Jubilee Oak go right down a track to make a short detour into Grinshill village, passing All Saints' Church. At the road go left - the Inn at Grinshill is a short distance ahead - and within a short distance go left again up

Gooseberry Lane. When the lane bends left go forward up a grassy path passing right of village hall to rejoin the enclosed bridleway on a sunken path soon with a stone wall left.

7 Within a short distance, when the route starts another ascent, at a marker post veer right to go ahead on a bridleway which follows the inside edge of woodland on a steady ascent. Pass a house to the right.

8 At the second property, at a fork, go left, up a stiffer gradient. Go left and ahead to continue the ascent. At the top of the climb, at a T-junction go right up a sunken path to retrace steps.

Grinshill and Corbet Wood

The Inn at Grinshill

6 Hope Bowdler Hill and Cardington

An exhilarating ridge walk, dramatic rock outcrops providing stunning views and a visit to one of the prettiest villages in Shropshire with a pub dating from the fifteenth century.

The mighty Caer Caradoc looms large on this walk although the route doesn't actually set foot on the hill. But the walk does soon gain higher ground to the rock outcrop of the Gaerstone to follow the ridge of Hope Bowdler Hill - now access land - with the most wonderful views. It's then over Willstone Hill, where the Battle Stones provide a stunning viewpoint, before a long gradual descent into Cardington. This delightful little village is mainly of local stone, but with the odd timber-frame property for good measure. The pub is a gem. The return is on an old drovers' road.

Level: 🥾 🥾 🥾
Length: 7.5 miles
Start: Large lay-by on B4371 at entrance to Gaerstone Farm one mile east of Church Stretton. Grid ref SO468932.
Terrain: Hilly with numerous ascents and descents on good grassy paths. A few boggy spots. Tracks and quiet lanes.
Nearest refreshments: The Royal Oak, Cardington 01694 771266. Choice in Church Stretton.
Recommended map: OS Explorer 217.

(map)

Church Stretton

B4371

Willstone Hill

Hope Bowdler Hill

Cardington — Pub

1000 m

35

Cardington Church

Cardington Church carving

1. From lay-by go right up farm road to pass Gaerstone Farm. Continue gentle ascent to pass through gateway with Caer Caradoc looming left. Within a few paces go right uphill with fence right to pass through corner gateway. Go half right up to join a footpath which goes ahead to crest the rise with a stile, right.

2. Do not cross the stile, but go left uphill to pass immediately right of Gaerstone rock. Now go ahead keeping to undulating crest of the long ridge of Hope Bowdler Hill to climb stile in facing fence.

3. Go forward on Willstone Hill keeping fence right. When fence veers off right - worth detour left for view from Battle Stones - continue

ahead, bearing slightly right. As descent gets steeper the path curves gently right to kissing gates.

(4) Pass through left-hand gateway and go left and ahead on field boundaries to North Hill Farm, continuing ahead on concrete road. When the road bends sharp left, turn right up a path and through two bridle gates and ahead on field edge. Pass through gates and go ahead bearing slightly left up field to top right-hand corner and through gateway going right to a road. Go left down lane.

(5) At The Villa Farm take the right-hand track. At a cottage bear left through a gateway and within a few paces, immediately after an old caravan, go left to a concealed stile. Go

Cardington Royal Oak

Cardington Churchyard

forward down field right-hand boundary. Ignore stile, right, and go half left and round end of high hedge and on to cross footbridge. Go ahead up to stile and cross field diagonally right, then left on enclosed path into Cardington. (Pub is right.)

6 Go left on road with church right. At T-junction turn right and within a few steps go left on No Through Road. At Old Vicarage bear right to go ahead through facing gateway to continue forward on field right-hand boundary. In far top corner go right through gateway to head up field right-hand boundaries eventually climbing a corner stile to go left to a road. Cross and go ahead on enclosed track at end of which go left to follow field edge - hedge left. After crossing second stile go ahead bearing gradually right to a stile and gate out on to an enclosed track

7 Go right to follow this old drovers' road - ignoring paths off. At far corner of clump of pine trees turn left and go forward on path which contours right and down to pass through bridle gate. Go half right on a low-level path which cuts a swathe through bracken at foot of Hope Bowdler Hill to pass through gateway at a house. Go left and ahead on a track to retrace steps.

The village of Cardington is a conservation area with a number of buildings dated from before 1600. The history of the Grade 2 listed Royal Oak Inn goes back as far as 1490 - even the water pump at the front of the pub is listed. The parish church of St James has a Norman nave and an Early English tower.

Willstone Hill

7 Lodge Hill and old mills by the stream

A gentle stroll to a good viewpoint before descending to a little river valley with sites of numerous water mills and a leaf out of a history book.

The Wesley Brook, which flows through a corner of East Shropshire,

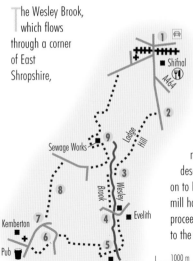

was once the power source for a series of water mills. This walk, from Shifnal, takes an easy-going ascent of Lodge Hill providing a wide view over the surrounding landscape with the neighbouring village of Kemberton in the near-view. The walk then descends to join the brook and on to Evelith where the impressive mill house remains. The walk proceeds through King Charles' Wood to the site of Kemberton mill and on

Level: ♥♥

Length: 6.5 miles

Start and parking: Shifnal. Car park off Aston Street signed in town centre from A464 Wolverhampton-Telford road. Grid ref SJ750077.

Terrain: Gently undulating on field paths, some over cultivated land. Quiet lanes.

Nearest refreshments: Masons Arms at Kemberton 01952 684019. Choice in Shifnal.

Recommended map: OS Explorer 242.

to Kemberton village. The return leg includes the site of a paper mill and finally a cottage reminder of the mill at Shifnal Manor.

1 Leave car park via alleyway alongside Co-op. At the end go left and straight ahead along Park Street. When the road bends left, go right on Park Lane.

2 Immediately after last houses on the right - row of white cottages - go right on a signed footpath which passes pond left. Keep on enclosed track as it bends left and goes ahead up field boundaries. Cross a stile and keep forward on gentle ascent of Lodge Hill, keeping to right-hand boundary. Crest the rise and walk downhill.

3 Climb corner stile and veer left on woodland path and down steps at the bottom of which go right to cross the brook. Turn left on a

Evelith

At Evelith Mill, after the future King Charles II had been defeated at the Battle Worcester in 1651, the fugitive prince was challenged by the miller and forced to make good his escape heading for the River Severn.

path which follows the stream - and can flood. Go ahead as the path crosses the bottom of a field and then continues forward on field edge with stream down to the left. Cross two stiles and through coppice to exit on to road at Evelith.

4 Go left on lane for about 100 yards passing the mill house, to turn right on a bridleway through King Charles' Wood. At T-junction go right to cross two footbridges and ahead to cottages. This is the site of Kemberton Mill. Go right on the unmade road – signed Kemberton. Immediately after passing through a gateway, go right (fingerpost) on hedged path.

5 At gated end go left over a stile and turn right on field boundary for 50 yards and go left at waymark to walk straight up the open field on a path which passes a power line post. Within a few paces of passing a solitary tree go right on a track.

Descent from Lodge Hill

Kemberton stream

Kemberton stream

King Charles' Wood

Do not pass through gateway, but go left and ahead on field boundary, followed by a green lane to exit on to a road. (This final section is not as OS map.)

6 Turn left passing a white cottage. Immediately before the next house go right and forward on gravel drive. Continue ahead on field boundary - ignoring kissing gate, right. Keep forward on enclosed path and immediately at the end of a wooden stable go right. Go left on field boundary up to a stile in top left-hand corner. Go ahead to exit on to a road in Kemberton. (Mason's Arms is straight ahead.) The direct route is right through the village.

7 Immediately after entrance to High Farm go left on enclosed track at the end of which continue ahead crossing two stiles. Go forward over a field bearing slightly left aiming about midway along the wide clump of trees. At field edge go ahead keeping trees immediately on your left for a few paces to a stile on the left. Cross and go half right down slope.

(8) At field edge go half right over field to pass through wide gap continuing forward bearing slightly left to a stile to a road. Go right keeping forward at junction. Ignore stile at gate, left, to continue on a descent keeping a track which bends sharp left (the site of a paper mill). A short distance before gated end turn left up a path.

(9) Go left on concrete road for about 10 yards, then right on a clear path to follow three sides of the sewage works to a kissing gate. Continue ahead on enclosed path which eventually skirts Manor Barns

Masons Arms, Kemberton

after which go left to follow access road passing Mill Cottage to exit on to a road at Shifnal. Go right on pave-

ment, keeping forward at island along Church Street. At T-junction go left to retrace steps to the start.

Evelith Mill

8 Lyth Hill

Enjoy sweeping views, with very little effort, from a countryside heritage site in an area which has strong links with romantic novelist Mary Webb.

When it comes to hill walks this one is really cheating! For with very little physical effort involved the escarpment of Lyth Hill - a countryside heritage site - provides a wonderful platform from which to view the south Shropshire landscape as it spreads out from the Wrekin in the east, to Caer Caradoc, the bulk of the Long Mynd and Earls Hill towards the west. The outward route follows the crest of the hill and although tempting to linger here, it is worth an extra bit of effort to step out leaving the dog-walkers behind and make a gentle descent towards Exford Green then to follow a green lane to Lyth Bank.

Level:
Length: 3.50 miles
Start and parking: Lyth Hill Countryside Heritage Site (first car park) a mile south of Bayston Hill signed off A49 four miles south of Shrewsbury. Grid ref SJ477072.
Terrain: Mainly level walking with only a few gradual gradients on field paths and tracks. One area in particular can be muddy.
Nearest refreshments: Pubs and shops in Bayston Hill.
Recommended map: OS Explorer 241.

The return follows field paths with views out towards Breidden Hills and Long Mountain on the Shropshire border with mid Wales.

1000 m

1 From first parking area go through the kissing gate and go forward on a path which follows the crest of Lyth Hill keeping the fence on your right. Ignore kissing gates, right, and carry on until the path runs out to pass through a gateway. Continue forward over another parking area with a toposcope and through a gateway to resume the walk on the footpath. Keep the path until this, too, ends at a gate.

2 Go left on an unmade road between cottages. Ignore a path, right, into woodland and continue forward through a gateway and ahead - ignoring path right - on a route which makes a gradual descent through gorse bushes. Pass through gateway and ahead to Exford's Green Venison Farm.

Welcoming sign

3 When the enclosed path ends, at the farm, go right up a bridleway which follows an enclosed unmade road, passing immediately to the rear of the farmhouse. Ignore a stile left and keep the bridleway to exit on to a road at Lyth Bank.

4 Go left down the road and at the junction veer right. After a few steps, immediately after the entrance to Westwinds, go right on narrow enclosed footpath. Cross a stile and go ahead on the field right-hand boundary with good views west including Breidden Hill and Long Mountain. Climb a stile and continue on field edge, crossing a footbridge and continue forward to pass through a gateway and ahead on a field-edge track.

A short distance from the start of the walk, on the crest of Lyth Hill, can be seen the squat remains of one of the few windmills in the county. Built in 1835 it was used for the preparation of hemp which was made into rope.

Toposcope on Lyth Hill

(5) Pass through next gateway and immediately go left through a pedestrian gateway. Veer right and ahead through a damp - and sometimes muddy - wooded area with stream left. Cross footbridge and go ahead on field edge with farm buildings right. Cross corner footbridge and continue forward passing two lonely stiles. Pass through corner gap and immediately go right out on to a farm road.

(6) Go right on the road keeping forward through Lythwood Farm yard and out on a track veering left at a fork to pass through a gateway. Continue ahead with fence right keeping the track as it bends left and goes ahead through arable fields. Pass through a gateway

Shropshire Way

and walk straight ahead over field to pass immediately to the left of an underground reservoir, and over corner stile to a lane. Go right back to the start.

Lyth Hill has associations with the early twentieth-century romantic novelist Mary Webb. Much of her work was set in her beloved Shropshire and it was while living in a cottage on Lyth Hill that she wrote House in Dormer Forest *and* Seven for a Secret.

View from Lyth Hill

Lyth Hill

9 Mucklewick Hill and Flenny Bank

A walk of ever-changing stunning views on footpaths over hills which are less frequented than the ever-popular neighbour - the rock-strewn quartzite Stiperstones ridge.

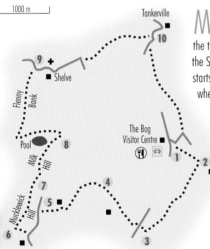

1000 m

Level: 🥾 🥾 🥾
Length: 8.75 miles
Start: The Bog car park on road from Pennerley to Bridges six miles north of Bishops Castle and east of A488. Grid ref SO358979.
Terrain: Three principal hills with fairly stiff gradients, field paths and tracks. Quiet lanes.
Nearest refreshments: The Bog Visitor Centre open mid-March to end of October Wednesday to Sunday and all school holidays. The Horseshoe at Bridges and Stiperstones Inn.
Recommended map: OS Explorer 216.

Mucklewick Hill, Milk Hill and Flenny Bank . . . just some of the treats in store on this walk in the Stiperstones area. The route starts from a site at a cross roads where once stood a thriving community with pub and school which developed in the eighteenth and nineteenth centuries to serve one of the numerous lead mines of the area. Today the only reminder of the past is the old school

- now a unique visitor centre well worth a visit - and a holiday cottage which was once the Miner's Arms.

Mucklewick Hill and Flenny Bank

(1) From top of car park take footpath signed Mucklewick Walk and Shropshire Way which rises to pass right of a pond at the end of which go left up sunken path to pass through a kissing gate. Go ahead keeping left of gorse bushes to pass through a kissing gate. Go ahead bearing slightly right over a field to a Shropshire Way finger post.

(2) Go right and ahead up the field to cross stile at left-hand corner of wood. Continue forward emerging to go ahead, crossing forest road and continue forward to climb a stile with Nipstone Rock right. Continue ahead on rock-strewn path.

(3) When level with rock outcrop turn right at a marker post.

Within a few paces go right and then veer left to follow waymarks to cross a lane and over a stile. Go forward turning left to follow road to Brookshill Farm. On approach to farm,

at a bend, go right over a stile, turn half left to go ahead over the field to climb a stile some distance right of a power line post. Go ahead up field boundary, hedge left.

Mucklewick Walk

Old lead mine

(4) In the corner continue forward on enclosed path at the end of which go ahead down a field with line of trees right. Within a short distance swing left to follow wheel tracks. Shortly after track bends sharp right, pass a building and immediately turn left over a stile to walk to left of a house, immediately turning right to walk in front of the property and ahead on a track.

(5) Within a short distance go left over a stile into a wood, down steps and over a footbridge. Go ahead up a field boundary to a lane. Go left and when lane bends left at farm buildings go right up unmade road. Pass through gateways and continue ahead.

(6) After a short distance go right (finger post) up a stony track for a short distance. When the track bends right continue forward uphill. Pass through bridle gate to enter access land and go ahead continuing to climb keeping a line of gorse bushes up to your right to walk on to a marker post. Continue forward through open land with a gentle slope on your right. The route continues forward to pass left of the summit of Mucklewick Hill - worth a detour for the view - to follow a wide grassy path which curves right

and ahead. Ignore bridleway, left, and continue forward on a descent.

(7) Climb stile at a gate and go ahead with trees, right, to follow a track then an old field boundary to continue forward keeping to crest of Milk Hill with Shelve Pool - a mining relic - down to the left. Continue forward between gorse and bracken to descend the hill at the foot of which go half right, crossing end of a track, and forward to cross a foot-bridge.

(8) Go ahead for about 50 yards then turn left over boggy ground to cross a ditch on a little causeway and ahead to climb a double stile now following Flenny Bank Walk signs. Go half left and

The volunteers who run the Bog Visitor Centre believe it is unique as being the only visitor centre to be lit by gas lamps. The centre is housed in former Victorian school which has retained its original interior with a real feel of stepping back in time. It is very much a walkers' haunt with muddy boots made welcome.
www.bogcentre.co.uk
or 01743 792484

ahead, cross footbridge, and head up the field gradually bearing left to field boundary with pool left. Cross stile in top left-hand corner and head up slope at top of which ignore facing stile and turn right, fence left. (In

valley left is Old Grit mine.) Walk forward along crest of Flenny Bank to eventually pass left of an established conifer plantation. Continue ahead bearing slightly left descending to pass through the left-hand gateway in corner to go ahead on an enclosed track to a road.

(9) Turn right to walk through Shelve. Pass a white farm-house and when the road bends sharp right continue forward over a stile and go ahead up field boundary, crest the rise and go left over a stile. Go ahead slanting slightly right aiming for a grassy hump - a tumulus. Cross stile in facing fence and go half right and at fence corner go right following fence to cross stile. Go ahead on field edge - hedge left. In corner go ahead

on enclosed path - with Tankerville mine left - to exit on to a road.

 Go right up hill to take the third track left - a bridleway.

The route now is forward - ignoring all roads and tracks off - initially on unmade road passing homes and then ahead on a track which passes offices of Natural England and a conifer plantation. Keep ahead to a road. Turn right to the car park.

Shropshire hill view

The Bog car park

10 **Wilderhope Manor**

From an enchanting Elizabethan manor house easy gradients lead to lovely views over a secluded valley.

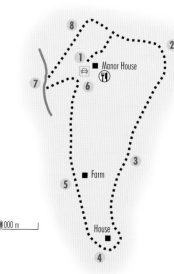

The sixteenth-century Wilderhope Manor stands on a slope of Wenlock Edge which stretches for nearly 16 miles from Much Wenlock to Craven Arms. The house is in the care of the National Trust and is used as a youth hostel. From the start this walk takes a gentle ascent through pasture to follow an elevated path - at times wooded - to give good views of Hope Dale and Brown Clee. The easy-going return follows a stream with the final leg giving options to shorten the walk

Level: ◆

Length: 4.75 miles for full circuit

Start: Wilderhope Manor signed off minor road from B4371 Church Stretton - Much Wenlock road at Longville in the Dale. Grid ref SO545929.

Terrain: Gentle gradients on field and woodland paths and tracks.

Nearest refreshments: Manor café open to non residents most days. Longville Arms at Longville in the Dale 01694 771206.

Recommended map: OS Explorer 217 Long Mynd.

Wilderhope Manor (National Trust and YHA) open April - September Wed and Sun 2-4.30pm. Oct - Jan Sun 2-4.30pm.

1 Facing the manor go left on a track signed Shropshire Way to Much Wenlock passing to the rear of the house. Keep hedged track to pass through a gateway and within a few paces go right over a stile. Go forward on field right-hand boundary with a pool, right. Cross corner footbridge and continue ahead on gentle ascent.

2 In the corner cross the first footbridge and stile, on the right, to go ahead up a field keeping a line of trees and old sunken path left. Pass through facing gateway and go forward keeping the same line to meet field boundary at right-hand corner of woodland. Turn right to walk up the field edge, hedge left. Climb stile in top corner - with the

Brown Clee view

Sheep everywhere!

first view of Brown Clee - and go ahead on a clear path which follows the inside edge of woodland, ignoring paths right.

 3 Emerge to cross a stile at a gate and go right down field boundaries. Keep to the field edge as the descent gets a bit steeper with a farm over to left. Pass a domestic TV aerial in a hedge and towards the bottom of the field follow the fence/hedge right - with a house right - to climb corner stile.

4 Ignore footpath over the bridge and go right to rejoin Shropshire Way. Bear left in the field and go ahead with stream left. Ignore footbridge, left, and keep forward. When a farm - Lower Stanway -

comes into view straight ahead ignore an old stone bridge, left, and go ahead to cross a stile. Continue forward ignoring another stream crossing to climb another stile. Go ahead on field boundary to cross stiles and old footbridge. Go forward on field edge to exit on to farm drive.

5 Go right, over stream and then left over a stile. Go forward on field boundary. Cross a stile, left, and footbridge and continue forward. Cross footbridge just left of field corner and go ahead up field edge with Wilderhope Manor ahead.

6 Cross a stile at gate in top corner. (Walk can be short-

Lake view

ened by going ahead.) For the extended route turn left through a gateway and go ahead on field edge. In the corner head up a tree-lined sunken path, veering right at fork. Pass through a gateway and go ahead, fence left, to join the access road at gate and cattle grid and go out to the road.

(7) Go right and immediately right on bridleway through woodland. When a five-bar gate bars the way turn right through a bridle gate to go forward on field boundary with woodland left. Pass through a side gate at double gates and continue ahead.

 At next gateway there is an option for a short cut by

MUCH WENLOCK
7¼ MILES

Much Wenlock finger post

going right immediately before the
gateway to descend on field edge
to the manor. For a few more views
continue ahead to pass through the
next bridle gate and immediately
go right down the field to meet a
track. Turn right to retrace steps
to the start.

Wilderhope Manor